Nobody Got Wet

A playscript
adapted from a story by
Roderick Hunt

by Jacquie Buttriss and Ann Callander

Characters

Narrator

Wilf

Wilma

Mum

This play has four speaking parts so that it can be read aloud in small groups. Sound effects can be added by children when they are familiar with the playscript but they have not been written in.

Narrator Dad got a boat.

Wilf Get in the boat, everyone.

Mum Push the boat out.

Wilma Dad is stuck.

Mum Oh no!

Narrator Mum pulled Dad.

Wilf Push the boat in, Wilma.

Narrator They went down the river.

Wilf Nobody got wet.

Mum What a good job!

Narrator They had a picnic.

Wilma It's raining.

Wilf But nobody is wet.

Narrator The boat floated away.

Wilma Look at the boat.

Mum Oh no. Help me get the boat.

Wilma Pull the boat in, Mum.

Mum Don't let me fall in.

Mum I didn't get wet.

Wilf Nobody got wet.

Wilma It's time to go home.

Everyone Oh no!

Narrator Everyone got wet!

The end

Printed in China by Imago